Tough Topics

Tobacco

Ana Deboo

Heinemann
LIBRARY

www.heinemann.co.uk/library

Visit our website to find out more information about Heinemann Library books.

To order:
☎ Phone 44 (0) 1865 888066
▨ Send a fax to 44 (0)1865 314091
▨ Visit the Heinemann Library Bookshop at www.heinemann.co.uk/library to browse our catalogue and order online.

First published in Great Britain by Heinemann Library, Halley Court, Jordan Hill, Oxford OX2 8EJ, part of Harcourt Education. Heinemann Library is a registered trademark of Harcourt Education Ltd.

Editorial: Charlotte Guillain
Design: Richard Parker and Q2A Solutions
Picture Research: Erica Martin and Ginny Stroud-Lewis
Production: Duncan Gilbert

Originated by Chroma Graphics (Overseas) Pte. Ltd
Printed and bound in China by South China Printing Company
ISBN 978 0 431 90775 8 (hardback)
11 10 09 08 07
10 9 8 7 6 5 4 3 2 1

British Library Cataloguing in Publication Data
Deboo, Ana
Tobacco. - (Tough topics)
1. Tobacco use - Juvenile literature 2. Tobacco use - Health aspects - Juvenile literature
I. Title
362.2'9

A full catalogue record for this book is available from the British Library.

Acknowledgements
The author and publisher are grateful to the following for permission to reproduce copyright material: Alamy Images pp. **10** (Oote Boe), **12** (Ace Stock Limited), **14** (Westend61/ Manfred J. Bail), **15** (Ace Stock Limited), **18** (Oso Medias), **20** (Gianni Muratore), **21** (vario images GmbH & Co.KG), **22** (Wm. Baker / GhostWorx Images), **23** (Realimage); Corbis pp. **8**, **17** (Buddy Mays), **25** (Robert Landau), **26**, **27**; Getty Images pp. **4** (Retrofile/George Marks), **5** (Photodisc), **6** (Photodisc), **7** (Photographer's Choice/Garry Gay), **19** (Stone/John Millar), **29**; The Kobal Collection pp. **9**, **24**; Science Photo Library pp. **11** (Pascal Goet-Gheluck), **13** (Alain Dex/Publiphoto Diffusion), **16** (Gusto), **28** (Doug Martin).

Cover photograph reproduced with permission of Corbis/ Zuma/Marianna Day Massey.

Every effort has been made to contact copyright holders of any material reproduced in this book. Any omissions will be rectified in subsequent printings if notice is given to the publishers.

Contents

Some words are shown in bold, **like this**. You can find out what they mean by looking in the glossary.

Smoking today

Sixty years ago, lots of people smoked tobacco. More than half the men in the United Kingdom smoked, and many women did, too. Since then we have learned how dangerous smoking is. Now far fewer people smoke.

◄ Smoking was very popular in the 1950s.

▲In the United Kingdom today, about one person out of four smokes.

Cigarettes are the most common way people smoke tobacco. Smoking cigarettes can give you bad breath, stain your teeth, and make your clothes and hair smell. Smoking is also bad for your health.

5

What Is Tobacco?

▲ China is the largest grower of tobacco in the world.

Tobacco is a plant that is grown in many parts of the world. It is related to plants that we eat, such as tomatoes, potatoes, and aubergines. It is also related to plants that contain poison.

Tobacco leaves are dried and used to make cigarettes, cigars, pipe tobacco, chewing tobacco, and **snuff**. All forms of tobacco contain a **drug** called **nicotine**.

◀ Many tobacco products are smoked.

Cigar

Tobacco's history

The first tobacco plants grew wild in North and South America. When Christopher Columbus arrived there in 1492, he saw how important tobacco was to the native people. European sailors tried tobacco, and its use quickly spread throughout the world.

◄ Native Americans smoked tobacco in some religious ceremonies.

◄ Early Hollywood stars often smoked in movies.

At first tobacco was too expensive for most people to buy. Then in the 1880s, a machine was invented that made cigarettes by the thousands. Suddenly many people could afford to buy cigarettes. By the 1950s, smoking was common in many parts of the world.

What happens when you use tobacco?

When someone uses tobacco, **nicotine** quickly enters the bloodstream. Soon it reaches the brain, where it causes special **chemicals** to be released.

▲Smoking can damage your sense of smell.

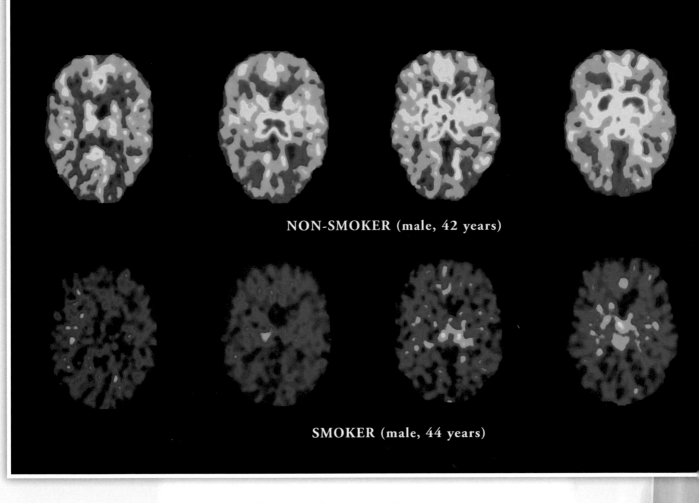

NON-SMOKER (male, 42 years)

SMOKER (male, 44 years)

▲ Smoking changes brain activity over time.

When nicotine sets these chemicals loose, they change the way the smoker feels. The smoker may feel more relaxed.

Tobacco addiction

◄ Smoking irritates the lungs and can make a person cough.

Many people do not like smoking the first time they try it. It can make them feel dizzy or sick. But **nicotine** is **addictive**. It makes people feel as if they cannot live without it.

At first, nicotine can make people feel good. When this begins to fade, people smoke more to bring the feeling back. Over time, smokers get used to nicotine and have to smoke more often for it to **affect** them.

▲Smokers may feel sick when the nicotine level in their body drops.

What is harmful about tobacco?

◄ Cigarette smoke releases a harmful chemical that is also used in rat poison.

Nicotine makes people keep using tobacco, which contains other harmful **chemicals**. One of the most harmful chemicals in tobacco is called benzene. It can cause cancer.

▲ **Carbon monoxide** gas is also given off by cars. It can be deadly in large amounts.

Tobacco smoke contains carbon monoxide, a dangerous gas. It is **absorbed** into the blood and takes up space that carries oxygen. This means smokers cannot breathe as well as they should. Their lungs and heart have to work harder and can be damaged.

Another harmful material in cigarettes is **tar**, the burned particles (pieces) in tobacco smoke. When smokers **inhale**, these particles go deep into their lungs and stick there. Tar can make it harder for smokers to breathe.

◄ Tar can cause diseases such as lung cancer and **emphysema**.

▶ People who chew tobacco have high rates of mouth cancers, gum disease, and dental problems.

Some people think chewing tobacco is safe because they do not inhale smoke when they use it. They do avoid **tar** and **carbon monoxide**, but the other **chemicals** in tobacco still get into the body.

How does smoking affect other people?

◄ Smoking risks the health of everyone around you.

For a long time, smoking was considered a risk adults took for themselves. Now it is known that people around smokers breathe in the same harmful substances. This is called **passive smoking**.

Passive smokers have a greater risk of lung and heart disease than people who do not live with smoke around them. Children are more likely to have lung problems such as **asthma** and **bronchitis** if they live with smokers.

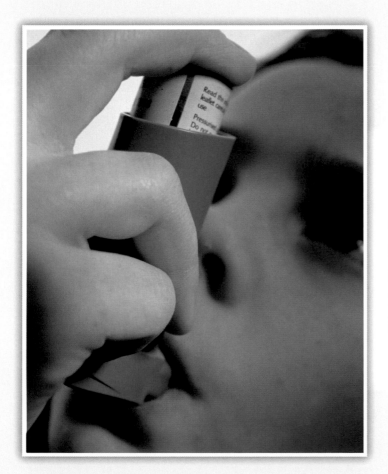

◀ People with asthma must sometimes use an inhaler to help them breathe.

Smoking and the law

Smoking is banned in all public indoor spaces in the United Kingdom. Smoking is also not allowed on aeroplanes in the United Kingdom.

▲Workers who are **addicted** to cigarettes have to take breaks to smoke outside.

▲ Smoking remains popular even though people know it is not good for them.

Selling tobacco products to young people is illegal. However, this law is not always obeyed. That means that young people often have to decide for themselves what is the right thing to do.

Why do kids smoke?

Smoking seriously harms you and others around you

Smoking kills

▲ Tobacco companies must include a health warning on cigarette packets.

Most people who smoke know that it can cause serious health problems. Still, a lot of young people try cigarettes and then become **addicted**.

Some young people start smoking because their friends do it. Some see family members smoking and want to know what it is like. Others may feel it helps them relax.

▶Young people may smoke because they think it makes them look older.

Tobacco companies

Tobacco companies know that smoking is dangerous. However, if they do not get young people to start smoking, the companies will eventually lose all their customers. Some tobacco companies try to make smoking look appealing to young people.

◄ The "Marlboro man" has been used to sell Marlboro cigarettes since 1955.

◄ Johnny Depp played a character who smoked on the television show *21 Jump Street*.

Many governments have banned television advertisements for cigarettes. As a result, cigarette companies have encouraged the creators of television programmes to use characters who smoke. That way, people see actors smoking and may want to start, too.

Trying to give up

◄ Few athletes smoke. They need strong, healthy lungs to perform well.

The sooner someone gives up smoking, the better. The heart and lungs begin to **heal** over time. However, many people try to give up several times before they succeed. It is important to keep trying.

Some people try to give up by first cutting down on the number of cigarettes they smoke each day. Smoking fewer cigarettes can make people **inhale** more deeply with each puff. This can be just as bad as smoking more cigarettes without inhaling as hard.

◄ Smoking fewer cigarettes does not always reduce the health risks.

Help with giving up

Giving up smoking can be difficult, but there are ways to get help. Special products that contain safe amounts of **nicotine** can help smokers give up. These include chewing gum and patches that are stuck onto the skin.

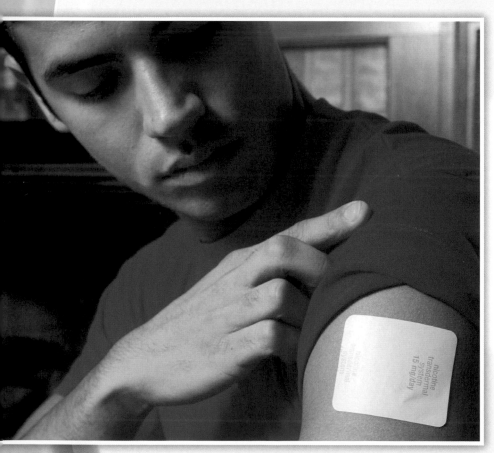

◄Patches give smokers the nicotine they need to help them give up smoking.

▶ "No Smoking Day" is held to remind people not to smoke.

Friends, family, and special organizations can help people who are struggling to give up smoking. Good places to look for information include Action on Smoking and Health (ASH) and the National Health Service (NHS).

Glossary

affect change

absorb soak in

addictive make a person feel as if they cannot live without it

asthma disease that can cause difficulty breathing

bronchitis swelling in the lungs that can cause breathing problems and severe coughing

carbon monoxide poisonous gas that is often created when something burns

chemical matter that can be created by or is used in scientific processes

drug something that is taken to change how the brain or body works

emphysema lung disease that can cause difficulty breathing and an infection in the lungs

flammable able to catch fire

heal get better

inhale breathe in

nicotine addictive chemical in tobacco products

passive smoking inhaling the smoke from other people's cigarettes

snuff tobacco product that is inhaled through the nose

tar small pieces of solid matter that make up cigarette smoke

Find Out More

Books to read

Talking about smoking by Bruce Sanders (Franklin Watts, 2003)

Harmful Substances by Cath Senker (Hodder Wayland, 2004)

Kate Smokes by Janine Amos (Cherrytree Books, 2002)

Websites

- The NHS has a site dedicated to helping people reject tobacco. (www.gosmokefree.co.uk)

- ASH offers information for people who are worried about smoking. (www.ash.org.uk)

- Quit is a charity that helps people give up smoking. (www.quit.org.uk)

Facts about tobacco

- **Nicotine** is named after Jean Nicot, who lived in the 1500s in France. He thought that tobacco would turn out to be a useful medicine.

- Many house fires are started when a smoker puts a lit cigarette too close to something **flammable**. Forest fires can be started when people throw burning cigarettes into dry grass.

- In the United Kingdom about 114,000 deaths every year are caused by the effects of cigarette smoking.

Index